FAST FOOD NATION

Based on the book by Eric Schlosser

Screenplay by Eric Schlosser
and Richard Linklater

LEVEL 3

Adapted by: Lynda Edwards

Fact files written by: Jacquie Bloese

Publisher: Jacquie Bloese

Editor: Tanya Whatling

Designer: Mo Choy

Picture research: Osha Hufton

Photo credits:

Cover: Cover art © 2008 Twentieth Century Fox Film Corporation. All Rights Reserved.
Pages 4, 5, 6, 7, 11, 13, 15, 16, 18, 21, 23, 26, 28, 29, 31, 35, 37, 39, 41, 43, 46, 48, 50, 52, 54 & 55: Courtesy of RPC Coyote Inc.
Pages 56 & 57: Penguin; D. Livingston/Getty Images; Twentieth Century Fox Film Corporation.
Pages 58 & 59: G. Bull, K. Lange/PA; AFP/Getty Images.
Pages 60 & 61: J. Haynes/Getty Images; A. Maslennikov/ Rex; Bettmann/Corbis.

Published by Scholastic Ltd 2009

Mary Glasgow Magazines (Scholastic Ltd)
Euston House
24 Eversholt Street
London NW1 1DB

Printed in Singapore. Reprinted in 2010.

CONTENTS

DON
Don is a marketing manager for Mickey's. He has to discover the truth about the meat in Mickey's hamburgers.

MIKE
Mike works at UMP. He finds jobs there for the Mexican workers. He likes Coco and Sylvia but he's a hard, unkind man.

RUDY
Rudy is a rancher. He hates everything about UMP.

COCO
Coco is Sylvia's sister. She goes to the USA with them. She's very pretty but she has a lot of problems.

SYLVIA AND RAÚL
Sylvia and Raúl are from Mexico. They are married and they're looking for a better life in the USA. But they have to go outside the law to get there.

ESTEBAN
Esteban guides the Mexicans through the desert and across the border into the USA. His job is very dangerous.

AMBER
Amber is a student who lives with her mum in Cody. She works at Mickey's in the evenings. She has big plans for the future.

CINDY AND PETE
Cindy and Pete are Amber's mum and uncle. They want Amber to have a good life.

PLACES

MICKEY'S
Mickey's is the name of big group of fast food restaurants. The business makes a lot of money.

CODY
Cody is a town in Colorado, USA. It has a lot of fast food restaurants, shops and a very big meat packing factory. A lot of Mexicans live and work here.

UNIGLOBE MEAT PACKING
UniGlobe Meat Packing (UMP) is a big factory just outside Cody. This is where cows are killed and their meat is used to make burgers.

FAST FOOD NATION

PROLOGUE

It was another sunny day in Cody, Colorado. A family got out of their car. They were ready for a meal.

'I'll have four Big Ones with chips.'

The girl smiled at the man and gave him four large burgers and chips.

'Thank you, sir. Enjoy your meal.'

He smiled and walked through the busy restaurant to his family. It smelt good!

They all loved Mickey's – they came here every weekend.

'Here we are guys!' he said, passing round the burgers. His wife looked up and smiled at him as the family ate. Life was good.

CHAPTER 1
'Don't kill the customer!'

Sylvia, her sister Coco, and her husband Raúl walked in silence through the dark, quiet streets. Sylvia held Raúl's hand tightly. She felt nervous and excited at the same time. It was their last night in Mexico. The border was just over fifty kilometres away. A new life in the USA was waiting for them, a life with a good future.

They reached a small house at the end of a street. Raúl turned to the women. 'Here it is. Come on.'

They went into a dark house and in the light of a fire they saw a small group of people. Esteban was waiting for them. He would be their guide through the desert and across the border. He looked at them. He didn't smile. He talked to the group.

'If one of you is weak, everyone is weak. If one of you is slow, everyone will become slow. Help your friends. Let's go.'

Raúl gave Esteban their money. They were on their way to a better life.

* * *

Mickey's was a large, successful fast food business. Inside its main offices a group of businessmen were in a meeting. They were talking about advertising. They were making suggestions about how to advertise their most successful burger.

'What about *The Big One only gets bigger!*' said one man.

'Or *Everyone wants a Big One!*' suggested another.

'How about *Eat me!*' laughed a third.

'OK!' smiled Jack, their boss. 'Good ideas! Now Phil, what have you got to tell us?'

Phil looked round the group. He was extremely pleased. 'It's amazing. We're selling more and more Big Ones. And all ages are buying them! Kids, adults, grandparents – everyone!'

'That's great. And Don, what about the Little Big Ones?' Jack turned to the newest person on the team.

Don also had good news. 'We did some tests and the kids really love them!'

'How many in a bag?' asked Jack.

'We think about three for a kid's meal.'

'Wonderful!' Jack was pleased. 'Dave – how about our plans to use the Teletubbies* to advertise the burgers?'

'Sorry, Jack. It's not going to happen. MacDonald's and Burger King have already got them.'

Jack's face went dark. '****!' he said.

* * *

Don was with Reilly, a scientist at Mickey's. There was a small, brown bottle on the table. Don put a piece of white paper in the bottle and then held it to his nose.

'Wonderful,' he said.

'That the Barbecue Big One,' said Reilly proudly. 'Does it need more smoke?'

'No. It's perfect. But this one …' Don smelt another

* A popular TV programme for very young children.

8

bottle, '… needs more of something.'

Reilly looked worried. 'The flavours in Caribbean food aren't easy.'

'Lime. Yes, a little more lime,' said Don.

Reilly smiled. 'No problem. I can add some more lime flavour. That's easy!'

* * *

Jack's secretary brought Don into his office.

'Good to see you, Don,' Jack smiled. 'So – what do you think of everything?'

'What does he want?' Don thought. He nodded and smiled. 'Everything's great, Jack.'

Jack got more serious. He spoke carefully. 'Don, we may have a little problem. Have you ever met Harry Rydell? He's at the Chicago office.'

Don shook his head. 'No, I don't think so. Why?'

'Harry's very successful. He gets the best price for the meat. But maybe he's too friendly with the guys who sell the meat. I think he's closing his eyes to some things they're doing.'

'What things, Jack?'

'Well, I have a friend who teaches food science. A couple of his students have tested some of our burgers. They found a lot of fecal coliform* in them.'

Don was confused. 'I'm sorry, Jack, I don't understand.'

'Manure, Don.' Jack looked directly at him. 'Or shit† if you prefer. There's shit in our burgers.'

* * *

* This is found in manure and it can make people ill.

† A rude word for manure.

The desert at night was beautiful. The low trees appeared blue in the moonlight. The Mexicans looked very small against the desert and the night sky. A young man called Roberto walked beside Coco.

'You have the wrong shoes for this journey,' he whispered. 'These are better. See? I got them in America. But I've got some cream if your feet hurt later.'

'Thanks,' said Coco. 'How many times have you done this journey?'

'Three. And you?'

'This is my first.'

* * *

It was getting late. Don finished reading a story to his sons and closed the book.

'Time for bed,' he said, and he kissed the boys.'

The next day he was travelling to Colorado to visit the meat packing factory. He was going to talk to Harry Rydell.

Don went into the living room. His wife, Debi, was at her computer. She looked at him.

'I don't understand,' she said. 'Why are they sending *you*? You're new.'

Don shook his head. 'Jack's worried. The meat is dirty and I've got to discover why.'

Debi's eyes opened wide. 'Dirty?'

'Yeah. Cow manure is getting into the meat.' Don still couldn't believe it. Manure in the burgers!

'That's terrible!' said Debi. She smiled at Don. 'So, it's a marketing problem. If kids eat your burgers and die, it's more difficult to sell them!'

Don smiled, but he wasn't feeling very comfortable. 'Yeah. It's an important rule in marketing. "Don't kill the customer!" It's bad for business.'

Chapter 2
Desert crossing

Coco was very tired. It wasn't easy to walk, and the sun was burning her face and arms.

Insects flew around her. 'Go away!' She shook her head and waved her arms angrily.

Roberto walked with her. 'Are you tired?' he asked softly.

Coco just looked at him. There was a question in her eyes. How much longer?

Behind them Sylvia and Raúl walked together. They didn't speak. Sylvia was trying to be brave. She knew this journey was really important. She looked across the desert. She tried not to think about the heat and the danger. She felt like a machine – one foot in front of the other, on and on.

The hot day turned to night and they continued the long walk to cross the border. There was no time to sleep or rest. They had walked through the heat of the day and now they walked in the black of night. Clouds covered the stars. The darkness was complete. But still they walked on towards their dream. They were tired and frightened, but they had hope.

* * *

Bright lights suddenly cut through the darkness. It was a car! Fear ran through the group like fire. They had to hide. Was it the border police? What would happen if they caught them?

Raúl and Sylvia hid behind a large rock. Sylvia could feel her heart getting faster and faster. No one moved. Was the car going to stop?

Finally, it passed and the fear passed, too. Sylvia felt weak. She smiled at Raúl in the darkness and pressed his hand. But where were the others?

'Coco?' she whispered.

Esteban's voice came out of the darkness, hard and sharp. 'She's here. Shut up!'

Slowly the people came out of their hiding places. They were all shaken. This was a dangerous journey.

Coco looked round. 'Roberto?' she called softly. But her friend wasn't there.

* * *

The night had passed. Roberto walked alone in the white heat of the sun. He stopped. The sand and grass looked the same in every direction.

Hot and tired, he took off his shirt and started to walk again. But where was he going? He had no idea. He was completely lost.

* * *

In another part of the desert, a vehicle appeared in the distance. This time no one ran. This vehicle would take them on the next part of their dangerous journey. They waited patiently by the side of the road.

It was a dirty, old, yellow van. It had words on the side that Sylvia couldn't understand. Benny, the driver, leaned nervously out of the window. He was small and dark. His eyes were hidden behind big sunglasses. He spoke quickly.

'Get in. Hurry up!'

Esteban opened the back of the van and the group climbed in. There wasn't much room in the van, but it was good to sit down after the long walk.

Coco was worried. Her chest felt tight. 'But what about Roberto? We should wait for him,' she said.

Esteban looked at her. It was too dangerous to wait. 'No. He knows the way.'

Benny was impatient. 'We're late and I'm leaving,' he said.

Coco's heart was heavy as she climbed into the van. She was afraid for Roberto. He was alone in the desert. What chance did he have? The van door closed loudly and shut out the sun.

* * *

Sylvia and Coco watched the desert through the window. They were getting nearer to their new life. Benny talked to them while he drove. He seemed friendlier now.

'Here's a present,' he joked, and he passed them bottles of water. It was the best water Sylvia had ever tasted.

Benny liked talking. When he was on the phone to his wife, he sounded like an American. Suddenly, he took something from his jacket. He held it out for the Mexicans to see. In the darkness in the back of the van, they could just see it – it looked big and heavy. It was a gun.

'A lot of people want to steal my cargo,' he explained. 'This is to stop them. It's my protection,' he said, and he waved the gun at them with a big smile. His teeth were very white.

Sylvia and Coco realised that they were his 'cargo'. They weren't people to Benny. They were his business. Sylvia, Raúl and Coco were trying to find a better life for themselves, but the men who helped them didn't care about their dreams. They only cared about money.

Benny stopped once to pick up more people and to let Esteban leave. Esteban was going back to Mexico to guide another group through the desert.

Benny read from a piece of paper. 'Who wants Canon City, Cody, Denver …?' He was taking the Mexicans to towns all over the USA.

Benny showed the new people his gun. This time he wasn't so friendly. Esteban had gone and he was alone with his cargo. He was a little man but the gun made him feel important. He waved it in front of their faces. 'Don't give me any trouble,' he said.

The van drove on through the night. The people were packed tightly together in the back. They tried to sleep, but excitement or fear kept them awake. Sylvia put her head on Raúl's chest. She could hear his heart. It was very loud.

* * *

Back in the desert, Roberto was getting weaker. His skin was burnt red and his lips were dry. He moved slowly. It was difficult to lift his feet. Around him he saw the desert through cloudy eyes. Nothing was clear any more. He knew he had to keep moving. He tried to push his feet forward one more time, but he fell heavily to the ground. After a short time he found enough strength to stand and walk a few more steps before falling again. This time he lay still and didn't get up.

CHAPTER 3
Welcome to Cody, Colorado

Don was enjoying the journey to Cody. He was driving through wide, open countryside and it was a bright, sunny day. Inside his car it was cool. Then he saw the cows.

The fields of green had changed to fields of brown. Thousands and thousands of cows were packed together behind fences. Don was amazed and got out to look. The cows were calm and quiet. They looked at him with big, dark eyes, like children. He realised that this was where Mickey's began. This was where the burgers started.

He drove on to Cody and stopped at the traffic lights. A dirty, old, yellow van stopped next to him. When the lights turned green, they drove off in different directions.

✳ ✳ ✳

The yellow van finally stopped and the back doors opened. Bright sunlight poured in. Sylvia, Raúl and Coco had arrived at their new home – a small, dirty room in a cheap hotel. Nine people crowded into the room. They stood or sat without talking. Their faces showed no feelings. Tiredness and shock made them silent. They waited.

Finally, the door opened and another man came in. This man was tall and strong. He was attractive, but his face was hard. He moved and spoke with confidence. His name was Mike.

Mike could speak Spanish, but he spoke to the Mexicans in English. He counted the people in the room and then he saw a man asleep on the floor. 'Stand up!' he said loudly. The man didn't move. Mike put his head close to the sleeping man. 'Stand up!' he said again. This time the others could hear the danger in his voice. The man woke and jumped up quickly.

Another Mexican was coming out of the shower. 'What do you think you are doing?' Mike said sharply. 'This is not a holiday!'

He looked at the frightened group and repeated the words slowly. 'This is not a holiday. Do you understand?'

He looked round the room, studying all the men. Which men were strongest?

He pointed at Raúl and another man, Jorge. 'You and you. In my truck, now!'

Sylvia watched Raúl go. She was very frightened, but she didn't show her fear.

Mike looked round the room again and his eyes rested on Sylvia for a moment. Then his look passed to Coco. He studied her face for several moments. Coco looked back at him directly. There was the touch of a smile in her eyes. Mike thought she was pretty. She liked that.

* * *

Don walked into his hotel room. It was bright and modern with a comfortable bed and a big bathroom. He switched on the television and unpacked his clothes carefully.

From his window he could see across the street. There was a Mickey's restaurant. Its lights were shining brightly in the dark night. 'Ah,' thought Don, 'that's where I'm going to eat tonight!'

* * *

'Are you ready to order?' The waitress smiled at Don. She was young and pretty. She was wearing yellow Mickey's overalls. Don noticed her name on the front: 'Amber'.

'I'll have the Big One.' Don smiled back.

It was late at night and he was the only customer. The restaurant looked bright and clean and the waitress was polite. She had a lovely smile. Don was pleased. This seemed a good place for Mickey's customers.

'What's your favourite thing on the menu?' he asked Amber.

'Oh, I like everything!' Amber laughed.

Don nodded. 'That's a good answer,' he said, and then explained, 'I work in Mickey's marketing department and I'm here to see where the Big Ones come from.'

Amber was interested. 'Really?'

'Did you know,' Don said, as he leaned closer, 'every Big One in the country is made at UniGlobe Meat Packing, right here in Cody?'

Behind Amber, in the kitchen, her friend Brian was preparing Don's burger. 'What a stupid guy,' he thought. Brian didn't like working at Mickey's and he didn't like the people he worked for either.

'Give me a burnt burger,' he said to the man who was cooking the meat. Then he put it in a box for Don. He smiled.

Don thanked Amber for the burger and took it over to a table by the window. He looked out at the traffic passing along the road and started thinking about the next day. Would he find anything bad at the meat packing factory? Was there really manure in the burgers?

* * *

Mike was driving Raúl and Jorge through Cody. The streets at night here were very different from the streets in Mexico. Raúl and Jorge couldn't believe their eyes. It was a new world for them. There were signs of money everywhere. This was a place for people who had lots of money. People here could buy everything they wanted. They passed fast food restaurants, supermarkets and shops. All of them had their names in bright lights. They had never seen anything like it.

Then the truck left the lights of the town and they started to pass more buildings – offices and factories. Finally, they arrived at a very large building with high fences and a guard at the gate. They saw the name 'UniGlobe Meat Packing' and a picture of a cow. Raúl looked at Jorge. They had arrived. This was the place where they killed the cows.

* * *

'Will we have to kill cows?' asked Jorge. He was in a changing room with Raúl. They put on special clothes: white boots, white overalls and gloves. Everything in the building was white, too. The ceiling, floors and walls were all completely white. It looked like a hospital.

Raúl shook his head. 'No. You need training for that. I don't know what we'll have to do. Wait and see.'

Without speaking, a man gave them hard, white hats to put on and special glasses. Then they followed him through the building. They passed many different rooms, but they couldn't see inside them. In one area men were pushing huge carcasses of cows. They were hanging from the ceiling and moved along special metal bars. Raúl had worked in many places before, but this place was different. It was clean and bright. There were people rushing everywhere. But no one spoke. It was like one big machine. Raúl noticed a man working in the corner. He only had one arm.

Then finally the man they were following pointed to a door. This was it. For a moment Raúl felt afraid. What was this work? Was it dangerous? Together, he and Jorge entered the room.

CHAPTER 4
The meat packing factory

Sylvia opened the hotel room door and smiled at Raúl.

'Good morning!' she said, happy to see him.

'Good morning,' Raúl said and tried to kiss her.

Sylvia moved back quickly. 'Oh!' She waved a hand in front of her nose. 'You smell!'

'Not as bad as the packing factory. That place smells *really* bad' Raúl replied. He moved past her into the room.

'What was it like?' Sylvia asked.

'I'll tell you after my shower!' Raúl kissed her quickly and laughed.

Sylvia and Coco waited outside for Raúl. They wanted to know about the job. They were excited and worried at the same time. Everything was so new and different. They didn't know what to expect.

Raúl joined them. Sylvia smelt his hair. She smiled. 'You smell nice!'

'What happened?' Coco couldn't wait.

'We had to clean the killing floor – where they kill the cows,' explained Raúl. 'We had big hoses like firemen have. There was blood and hair and bits from the dead cows all over the floor and we cleaned it with hot water from the hoses.'

'No!' The girls were shocked.

'And the water was so hot we couldn't see through the plastic glasses. We had to take them off.'

Coco's eyes were wide. 'That's terrible!'

Raúl nodded. He touched Sylvia's arm. 'But don't worry, you won't have to do that. You'll probably be in the room where they cut up the meat. That's easier.'

Sylvia was still worried. 'Were they nice to you?' she asked.

Raúl looked down. 'No, but …' Then he smiled, 'that's not important. Look!'

He handed Sylvia the money from his pocket. The girls' mouths fell open in surprise. It was eighty dollars! In Mexico you had to work for weeks to earn eighty dollars. They all laughed. Their dream was coming true!

* * *

Don's visit to the packing factory was going very well. Everywhere was extremely clean and he liked that. The workers looked busy and happy. That was good, too.

His guide, Terry, was clearly very proud of the place. He showed Don everything from the cut meat to the boxes of burgers. Machines did the cutting and made the meat into round burgers. Then the burgers went through a machine like a big freezer. Then people packed the burgers into boxes. Thousands of boxes were ready to go on the trucks. Everything was very quick and very clean.

Don was amazed. 'That's a lot of Big Ones!'

Terry smiled. 'People all over the country are going to eat these tomorrow night.'

Don was happy to see that everything looked so clean. There was no sign of manure anywhere. Perhaps there wasn't really a problem. Perhaps Jack had got the wrong information.

Just before he finished his tour of the factory, Terry showed Don a room full of new workers. They were watching a video about safety at work.

'Safety is very important here,' he said seriously. 'All new workers must watch this safety film.'

'Excellent!' thought Don. That was another good point for the packing factory.

He didn't realise that the workers were Mexican and the film was in English. They didn't understand a word.

* * *

Sylvia and Coco sat together watching the safety film. They had no idea what it was about. They didn't know the language and the pictures moved very quickly.

When they left at the end of their first day at work, Sylvia felt tired and unhappy. Coco, however, was strangely excited. She was watching Mike. He was shouting at two Mexican men who were standing by his truck.

'I like him,' she said.

'Who, Mike?' Sylvia couldn't believe it.

'Yeah, I think he's cool.' Coco smiled to herself.

'You're crazy!' Sylvia said, and turned away.

Coco could see that she wasn't happy.

'What's the problem?' she asked her sister.

Sylvia didn't answer. She was upset and she was thinking about the packing factory. Finally, she spoke. 'That place is horrible. I don't want to go in there ever again. There's got to be another job.'

CHAPTER 5
'We're all just part of the machine'

'The Big One's a great success. Sales are getting better and better.' Amber's boss, Tony, was talking to Don at a table in the empty restaurant.

'Yep. It's the same everywhere.'

Don drank some coke. He felt good. Tony seemed a nice guy. But he had to ask him about the packing factory. 'So, have you ever been out to the UMP?'

Tony shook his head. 'No. Why?'

Don played with his glass. 'Er, it's just … I've heard some bad things about the place. I wondered …'

Tony nodded. 'Yeah, I've heard some bad things, too.'

Don's eyes opened wide. He hadn't expected this. 'Like what?' he asked quickly.

Tony looked uncomfortable. 'Just some stories.' He looked down at his hands. 'A long time ago a friend of mine worked there. They probably weren't true.'

Don was worried. 'I was there today. It looked really clean.'

Tony didn't look at Don. Perhaps he'd said too much. 'It's probably different now.'

'Can I speak to your friend?' Don asked.

'He's not there now. But …' Tony wasn't sure. Was this a good idea or not? The stories might be true. Don needed to know.

He decided. 'You can talk to my wife's uncle, Rudy, if you want. He's a rancher. He used to sell cows to them. He knows a lot about the place.'

'And will he talk to me?'

Tony smiled and looked directly at Don for the first time. 'He won't stop,' he said.

Mike was angry.

'What are you doing?' he shouted at a woman in the meat cutting room. 'That's the best meat. You don't put it with the cheap bits. If you do that again, I'll put you on the killing floor. Understand?'

The woman's face was pale. She nodded quickly. There were tears in her eyes. 'Yes, yes,' she said.

Further along the line Coco was cutting meat, too. Mike's eyes turned to her. He walked slowly down the line of women and stopped behind her. She felt his hand on her leg. She looked at him shyly and smiled.

'What's your name?' he whispered.

'Coco.'

'Sweet Coco,' he said, and then moved on.

A woman working beside Coco was watching. 'Be careful of him,' she whispered. 'He likes all the pretty girls. He gives them drugs.'

Coco's eyes followed Mike as he walked down the room. He was big and strong. 'A bad guy, huh?'

The woman nodded. 'Honey, he's the worst.'

* * *

Later that night Mike gave Coco a ride in his truck. He stopped in a lonely place. Then he kissed her.

* * *

Don lay on the bed in his hotel room. He was talking to his wife on the phone.

'I think I'll be home on Saturday,' he told her. 'I'm going out to a ranch and then I'm seeing Harry for lunch. Say "Hi!" to the boys.'

Two women came in to clean the room. They stopped in the doorway when they saw Don lying on the bed. One of the girls was Sylvia. Don just waved his hand and the girls backed out of the room.

Sylvia was worried. Was the man angry? Had they done the something wrong? She had decided to work in the hotel and not the packing factory. The money was worse but the job was better.

'Don't worry!' said Vicky. She had worked at the hotel for a long time.

'It's good you came to work here,' Vicky continued, while they tidied another room. 'UMP is a bad place. I worked there for a few weeks. There's blood everywhere and it's dangerous. You can lose a finger or a hand in those machines.'

Sylvia's eyes opened wide.

'Tell your husband to leave,' Vicky said.

* * *

Don was nervous about his meeting with Rudy, the rancher. What would Rudy tell him about the factory? He waited by the gate to the ranch and looked around. There was grass as far as he could see. He saw an old car coming towards him. It stopped and a man got out. Rudy wasn't young, Don realised, but strong and active. He lived a healthy, outdoor life.

'Are you the one who wants to talk about UMP? Get in.' Rudy's intelligent blue eyes looked straight at Don.

Don climbed over the gate with difficulty. He didn't do much exercise.

They drove for a long time. 'Is this all your land?' asked Don, amazed.

'Yeah,' said Rudy. 'But look at this.'

He stopped the car. At the edge of the grasslands were hundreds of new houses. 'Those are my new neighbours. Life's changing, Don. Ranchers are losing their lands. Everyone wants it for building.'

They got back in the car and Rudy drove them up to his old ranch house. 'I'm not a real rancher anymore,' he told

Don. 'The old way of life is disappearing. I don't know about you, but I don't like this new one.'

* * *

Don and Rudy sat together in Rudy's ranch house. It was comfortable. A big fire warmed the room.

Don finally asked the big question, 'What do you know about UMP?'

Rudy looked at him and thought for a moment. 'A lot,' he said. 'Those guys are mean. They care about money and nothing else. They destroyed my grandfather's business – he used to sell cows to them. They'll do anything to get cheaper meat. Anything.'

Don still couldn't believe it. 'But do you think they really sell us dirty meat?'

Rudy sat back in his chair and laughed. 'Of course they do. All the time. Those guys – they don't care when workers' hands and arms are cut off by the machines. They're not going to worry about manure in the meat!'

'But I saw the factory. It was clean.' Don didn't want to hear this.

'Did you see the killing floor?'

Don shook his head. 'I don't think so.'

'Did you see the bloody carcasses and walk across floors covered in blood?'

Don was shocked. 'No.'

'Then they showed you nothing.'

'But how …,' Don started to ask.

'Rita!' Rudy called out.

A smiling Mexican woman came into the room. She looked after the house for Rudy.

'Rita,' said Rudy, 'tell Don about UMP.'

'My brother works at UMP,' said Rita. 'He tells me things. The big problem is the conveyor belt – it moves so fast. The workers can't clean the carcasses well. They don't have enough time. Sometimes they pull the stomach out and they make a mistake. Then manure goes all over the meat.'

Don's mouth felt dry. 'But how often does this happen?'

'Every day,' said Rita.

'You see, Don,' Rudy explained, 'it's like I said. This is a new life. The machine's the boss now. We're all just part of the machine. When it's finished with you, it moves on and uses someone else. And another thing,' Rudy added, 'you're a nice guy, but your burgers are awful. And that's not only because they've got manure in them.'

CHAPTER 6
Harry Rydell

Don was having lunch with Harry Rydell.

He looked at the burger in his hand. The meat was brown and shiny. Suddenly, he wasn't hungry anymore.

'You like your burger, Don?' Harry asked.

He took a huge bite from his burger and wiped the tomato sauce from his mouth. He was a big man and he talked all the time. His eyes were clever and hard. Harry Rydell was a good businessman.

'Yeah, thanks Harry.'

Now Don had to ask difficult questions. He put down his burger. 'Harry, what's going on at UMP?' His face was serious.

'Sorry?' Harry stopped eating for a moment.

'I've been talking to people, Harry. They're trying to move things too quickly. Workers are getting hurt – one guy lost his arm!'

'Yeah?' Harry looked at Don.

'And Harry, there's manure in the meat.' Don sat back, his hands on the table.

'Really?' Harry bit into his burger again.

He thought for a moment and looked at the burger. Then he looked back at Don. 'You know Don – there's probably a little bit of manure in this burger. There's always been dirt in our food. We all have to eat a little dirt sometimes.' He continued eating.

Don was getting angry. 'Your tests showed the meat was clean, Harry.'

Harry spoke slowly and calmly. 'Everything's fine, Don. You just have to cook the meat well. That's the problem with Americans today. They're afraid of a bit of dirt!'

'So, you knew about this?' Don was shocked.

Harry looked at Don coldly. He didn't answer his question. 'Have you ever been to Mexico? It's a beautiful country. But the people there are really poor. Those guys come here to get a better life and they work hard for it. I like that. Don't you?'

Don shook his head. 'Harry, I have to tell Jack about this.'

Harry took another bite of his burger. He didn't look worried. 'Take my advice, Don. You seem a nice guy. Be careful. Jack's in trouble, big trouble. He's been stealing from the company. Maybe in two months he'll be out.'

Don couldn't believe it. He liked Jack a lot. 'But …'

'Don,' Harry explained patiently, 'I get really cheap meat for Mickey's. The cheapest. Without me, there wouldn't be a Big One. Now, I understand what you're saying. Perhaps there *is* too much manure in that meat. So, I'm going to go over there and get angry with a few people. I'm going to do that for you.' He smiled at Don.

Don shook his head. 'That's not going to be enough.'

Harry's smile disappeared. 'Don, Don ...You know, I'd hate to see you in trouble. Think about the future, Don. Think about *your* future.'

* * *

Don sat in the dark in his hotel room. He felt terrible. He didn't know what to do. Should he tell Jack? Should he keep quiet?

He phoned Debi. 'Honey, this is a real problem. I'm certain something's wrong. But I could lose this job. I could lose it if I say something and I could lose it if I don't.'

He listened to her reply. She was worried, too. He leaned back and closed his eyes. They had to pay for the house, they had to think about the children ...

'I know, honey,' he said, '*I* don't want to move again either.'

He put the phone down and went to the window. Outside, Mickey's restaurant was closed, but the lights on the sign were still shining brightly. Don thought everything looked plastic and empty now. He felt sad and very tired. What should he do?

* * *

'Jack, I think everything's OK.' Don tried to sound cheerful on the phone. 'I talked to lots of people. I even went out to see a rancher who knows the place well ... Yeah, I talked to Harry, too. Interesting guy! But I think he's honest ... OK. Perhaps we need to do some more tests in the future. But for the moment ...'

* * *

Don went to pay his bill. He felt very tired and his heart was heavy.

'You made four phone calls.' The girl was young, pretty and bright.

'Yes.'

'And you rented three films.'

'That's right.'

'Did you enjoy your stay with us?'

She sounded like a machine. She probably said exactly the same things to every customer.

He wanted to shock her a little. 'No, not really,' he said.

What would she say now?

'That's good,' she continued. 'I hope you stay with us again soon.'

Don paid and walked slowly out of the hotel. He wasn't very proud of himself. He didn't like what he was doing.

Chapter 7
'Hope can kill you'

Raúl and Sylvia had been in Cody for a month. They decided to go out for their first meal in a fast food restaurant. Sylvia held Raúl's hand tightly as they crossed the busy roads. Everything was so fast. She and Raúl felt very small in this big, new world.

They ordered Chinese chicken and cokes. The waitress smiled as she wrote it down. Sylvia felt uncomfortable. She realised they couldn't really understand the menu. After the meal they walked hand in hand along the road, looking at the shops.

Raúl was happy. He was beginning to feel at home here.

'That was fantastic!' Raúl laughed. 'Look,' he said, pointing at a car for sale, 'I'm going to have that one when we have the money.'

Sylvia was quiet. She smiled. Raúl felt that she wasn't as happy as him. 'Are you OK?' he asked.

'I'm fine,' she said, and smiled again.

But she wasn't fine. Something was wrong in this new life, but she didn't know what. She felt a little afraid of the future.

* * *

When Raúl opened the door to the flat, he heard Sylvia and Coco shouting.

Coco's face was red. She was very angry. 'You're not my mother!'

'You're out all night! You take drugs! I'm worried about you, Coco.' Sylvia's face was pale.

'It's my business, not yours.' Coco turned away. She didn't want to listen.

'Look at you!' shouted Sylvia. 'You don't eat – you're going to be ill.'

'You're upset because my life is better than yours!' Coco's face was ugly. 'My boyfriend is …'

'He's not your boyfriend,' Sylvia said, angrily.

'You wait six months. Then we'll see who is doing better, you or me!'

Raúl stepped between them. 'OK, OK. Calm down.' He raised his hands.

Coco ran out of the flat. She was crying and laughing at the same time. 'You wait!' she shouted.

Sylvia didn't know what to do. 'Raúl, she's going to get into big trouble.'

Raúl turned away. 'She's not the only one. A lot of people take drugs there. It makes the work easier.'

'So you think she's right?' Sylvia couldn't believe it.

Raúl went into the bedroom and shut the door.

Outside, Coco tried to phone Mike. He didn't answer.

* * *

'Uncle Pete!' Amber was excited. She hadn't seen her uncle for a long time. Now here he was in their living room when she came home from Mickey's. What a wonderful surprise!

Pete laughed. He cared a lot about his niece and Cindy, her mother. He looked at them laughing together. Cindy looked more like Amber's sister than her mother. But he noticed that Cindy looked tired. Their life was difficult. Cindy never had enough money.

He pointed at Amber's bright yellow overalls. '*What* are you wearing?'

'I've got a job!' Amber knew he didn't like Mickey's.

'Cover it up! That's a terrible place!' He tried to put a coat in front of her and they all laughed again.

'Hey, you two,' Cindy said, 'I have to do a few things. Why don't you go out for the evening?'

Pete smiled. 'Good idea. But only if you change those clothes, Amber. I'm not going out with a banana!'

* * *

Amber went with Pete to The Cooler, a popular bar in Cody. It was full of students talking and laughing and having a good time.

'You used to like Mickey's,' Amber looked at him

over her glass. 'You took me there when I was a kid. I remember.'

Pete nodded. 'I liked the first one. Now there are – what – 400?'

'Well, I needed the job,' she explained. 'But I'm not going to stay at Mickey's all my life. I've got plans.'

Pete was pleased. 'So, what do you want to do?' he asked.

Amber looked round The Cooler at all the students. 'I want to go away to college. Maybe Montana?'

Pete smiled and started writing on a piece of paper.

'And I want to be an aeronautical engineer*,' Amber continued.

Pete gave her the piece of paper. Amber read: 'No babies before 21 and I will give you $1,000.'

She laughed. 'I agree. No babies!'

Pete was serious. 'You know, I read a story in a paper once. It said that the happiest people are the people who follow their dreams. Even if they don't succeed – they feel good because they've tried.'

Amber nodded. 'I can understand that.'

'So,' Pete continued, 'that means: don't listen to me or your mom or anyone else. Listen to yourself. If you listen to other people, you'll be in the same cage as a million others. You don't want to be like that.'

* * *

'So, is Cody a better town today or when we were kids?' Pete asked his sister.

They were back at the house. They were talking about modern life.

Cindy had different ideas to Pete. 'I think it's OK. It's bigger and there's more to do.' She sat down.

* A person who designs engines for planes.

Pete laughed. 'Yeah, you've got Arby's, Denny's, Mickey's, Wendy's, Chilli's, Appleby's, Hardee's* …'

Cindy hit him with her handbag. 'I know, I know. The world is ending. Big business is killing us all! Look,' she stood up to get a coffee, 'I don't have time for all your politics. And you're too old to do anything about it anyway!' She went into the kitchen.

Pete shook his head. 'See, Amber? It's the young people who have to change things. You must try to change things when you're young or it'll be too late. Look at me and your mom.'

Cindy came back into the room. 'And don't copy your uncle, young lady,' she said. 'He was part of a student protest at college and he had to leave. Dad had to pay the lawyer $2,000!'

Pete put his hands up. 'OK, OK. The college had business in South Africa. Students all over America were protesting about the government in South Africa in the 80s.'

'So, what happened?' Amber was interested. She didn't know about her uncle's past.

* These are popular fast food restaurants.

'Well, the police came. I had to leave college. But a year later the college stopped putting money into business in South Africa.'

'What's your point, Pete?' asked Cindy.

'If everyone does a little bit, then perhaps we can change things. Perhaps we can make a better life.'

Cindy drank some coffee. 'I hope things get better, I really hope so.'

'Don't hope.' Pete was serious. 'You can't just hope. You've got to *do* something. In a town like this, hope can kill you.'

CHAPTER 8
Who's in control?

Coco felt ill. Her skin was hot and her head was heavy. It felt like there were clouds behind her eyes. She wanted Mike. No, she didn't want him – she needed him. She needed his little packets of drugs. But he wasn't answering her calls. Was he tired of her? Had he found someone else?

She tried to work. She held the knife in her hand. She cut the meat into small pieces and threw it onto the conveyor belt. She did it again and again, like a machine. She felt terribly tired. Then she saw him.

Mike had come into the cutting room with Maria, another worker. They stood very close together and Maria had a smile in her eyes. Suddenly, Coco felt hot white anger rise inside her. She took her knife and walked slowly across the room to face Maria.

Coco's voice was low and hard. 'Don't you go near him again – *ever!*'

'And what are you going to do about it?' Maria smiled.

The clouds behind Coco's eyes turned red. She lifted the knife. She wanted to kill Maria. She mustn't steal Mike from her. He was her life, her future.

Suddenly, Mike's hands were pushing Coco's arms. 'Are you crazy?' he shouted. 'Go back to work! You want to fight – then fight in your own time. Not at work.'

He pushed Coco back to her place in the line and put his mouth to her ear. 'If you slow the work on the line again, you're out!'

Behind his back, Maria smiled at Coco and shook a finger at her. The other women were enjoying the entertainment. Work had stopped. 'Back to work, everyone,' Mike said angrily.

Coco stood in her place quietly. She had no feeling. She was empty. She watched the pieces of meat move along the belt. She couldn't think. Why couldn't she think? And what was that ringing sound in her head? She suddenly felt very weak and her arms and legs refused to move. The room started turning. Coco fell to the floor.

* * *

'She needs more sleep,' said the nurse when Mike came into her office.

Coco sat on a chair looking very pale. There were dark circles under her eyes.

'She's got another hour at work,' Mike said.

The nurse nodded. 'She'll be OK.'

Mike took Coco out of the room. They walked back to the cutting room. 'You've been a bad girl,' he said quietly.

Coco turned to him quickly and pulled his head

towards her. She looked into his eyes. 'If you touch Maria again, I'll *kill* you,' she whispered.

Mike started to laugh but then stopped. Coco was deadly serious and there was something dark and dangerous in her eyes. He took her into a small room and locked the door. Coco reached up and kissed him.

'Listen,' he said, between kisses, 'me and Maria – it's not your business. I know you're tired. I'll find you another job. Something easier, OK?' Coco took the small packet from his hand. The clouds behind her eyes started to disappear. Life was good again.

* * *

'Life was good,' thought Amber. She wasn't working tonight. She was with her friend Kim at The Cooler.

A pretty blonde girl and a young man with a serious face came over to their table. 'Hi!' said the girl. 'You were here a few nights ago, weren't you?'

'Yes, that's right.' Amber remembered she had seen them before.

The girl smiled. 'I'm Alice and this is Andrew. Look – we're going to a party later. Do you want to come? It's going to be cool.'

Amber looked at Kim. A party! 'Sure. Why not?'

* * *

Amber was enjoying the party. Alice and Andrew were interesting and they had strong opinions about many different things.

Andrew was talking about big businesses and what they do to the environment. 'They lie all the time and we believe them.'

'There's a book, *Crimes Against Nature*. You must read it,' Alice told them. 'These companies – they're cutting down the trees. They say it's to keep the forests healthy.'

Andrew laughed. 'How crazy is that? And they tell us that the air is clean now. It's all lies.'

Amber listened. They were right. Why hadn't she realised it before? Mickey's and companies like Mickey's were hurting the world, not helping it. And they wanted to control everyone so that they could continue. She had to hear more.

* * *

'I'm sorry, Tony.' Amber looked uncomfortable, but she had to do this. 'I can't work here any more.'

Tony couldn't understand. 'But you're a good worker, Amber. You can do well here at Mickey's.'

Amber looked at her hands. 'It's not because of you, Tony. It's because this isn't real – Mickey's isn't real.'

Tony's eyes went cold. 'OK,' he said. 'If that's what you want. Goodbye, Amber.' He turned away.

Amber wasn't sure what she wanted, but it wasn't Mickey's. She walked out of the door for the last time.

CHAPTER 9
A terrible accident

The killing floor was filled with noise. Huge machines were turning. Hot water poured out of the men's hoses. It hit the walls and floor at high speed. The water reached every corner of the room and every part of the machines. Blood and bits of meat washed across the floor. The men were dangerously close to the deadly teeth of the machines. They had to clean everything.

Suddenly, one noise cut through all the others. It was a scream – a man's scream.

Raúl looked across the room. What had happened? His heart stopped. He saw that his friend Francisco had fallen into the mouth of one of the machines. Raúl could see his white fingers. They were holding on to the side of the machine while the teeth bit into Francisco's legs. Raúl and Jorge ran over and held onto Francisco's arms. They couldn't pull him out because the machine was still turning. There was blood everywhere. One of Francisco's legs was gone. Still the machine was turning. Why wasn't anyone stopping it?

'Turn it off! Turn it off!' Raúl shouted over the noise. He needed all his strength to hold on to Francisco. Then suddenly the machine stopped and Raúl fell backwards off the platform. He landed heavily on his back two metres below. His body was filled with a terrible pain. He tried to get up, but he couldn't. Raúl couldn't move his legs.

* * *

Sylvia sat alone and afraid in the empty hospital waiting room. What had happened? Was Raúl OK? Finally, a man in a dark suit came to speak to her. There

was a woman with him to help with the language problem. The man was from UMP and his face was serious.

'Is he OK?' whispered Sylvia, her eyes full of hope.

'Well,' explained the man, 'he's in a lot of pain, but he's not going to die. The worst problem is his back. But it's possible that he had that problem before the accident.'

Sylvia listened carefully while the woman explained in Spanish. When she heard the words 'not going to die' her heart lifted. But the man had more to say.

'I'm afraid his blood test showed drugs,' he shook his head. 'They probably caused the accident.' Again Sylvia waited for the woman to explain.

'That's not true!' she cried when she understood. She couldn't believe it.

'You can check the tests,' the man said quickly. 'Drugs are not allowed at UMP. The accident wasn't our fault. I'm sorry.'

He had done his job. He made sure that Sylvia understood. Raúl would get no money from UMP. He left.

Sylvia's heart was breaking. 'What is going to happen now?' she thought. 'Raúl can't work. We have no money. Our lives are finished.'

* * *

'I'm sorry, Coco. I was wrong to get angry with you.'

Sylvia was sitting in Coco's flat. It was clean and bright with nice, modern furniture. Coco was looking better now.

'It's forgotten,' she said, and she put her arms round her sister. 'I'm so sorry about Raúl. I'd like to help you, but I have to pay for my new car.'

Sylvia shook her head. 'No. That's OK. But I need a job at UMP. Can you arrange that?'

Her face was pale. She didn't want to do this, but she had no choice.

'I'll call Mike,' Coco promised. 'He got me a job in the office. Perhaps we can work together.'

'That would be good,' Sylvia said quietly.

* * *

'We have problems at UMP,' Mike explained. He wasn't optimistic about a job for Sylvia. 'It might have to close. The place is costing too much money. I love your sister, but I don't know if I can help you.'

He looked at Sylvia. He thought she was very pretty. Sylvia's eyes were empty. She knew what he wanted. She moved closer as Mike leaned down and kissed her.

CHAPTER 10
Amber's beautiful idea

Amber sat and listened in silence. She was amazed. Alice, Andrew and some other students were discussing environmental problems. These were important things, serious things. Why had she never thought about them before? 'I've been asleep most of my life,' she thought.

Her new friends cared deeply about the world and its problems. They asked lots of questions. Amber felt alive when she was with them.

'There are about a hundred thousand cows outside Cody,' Andrew's eyes were bright. 'The cows pollute the air and the rivers with their gas and manure. It's a huge problem.'

Alice leaned forward, 'It's a terrible life for the cows,' she added. 'They're packed together behind fences. It's like a prison for them. You can smell the place three miles away.'

Amber followed the conversation carefully. This was shocking.

Andrew spoke again. 'We're going to write a letter,' he said importantly. 'We …'

Another student, Paco, stood up suddenly. He looked at Andrew angrily. 'A *letter*? Are you crazy? You can't do anything with a letter!'

Paco wanted change and he wanted it quickly.

Amber suddenly had an idea. She was excited.

'There are a hundred thousand cows. If we cut the fences, they'll all run free. We'll get people's attention.'

The other students looked at her. Paco smiled slowly. 'That's beautiful, Amber, beautiful!'

Andrew wasn't happy. 'You know that's against the law. You can go to prison for a long time.'

Amber was getting more confident. 'Imagine it! Thousands and thousands of cows, all going back to their homes on the grasslands. There will be cows on the roads, traffic problems – people will have to notice!'

'Then we'll write to the papers.' Alice loved the idea. 'We'll explain why we did it. We'll tell the company what to do!'

Andrew was worried. 'But the government …'

No one was listening to him.

'Let's do it!' said Paco.

Amber looked at him and smiled.

* * *

The cows were usually calm at night. But not tonight. They could smell something different in the air. They moved their heads from side to side and made low calling sounds. There was a strange noise in the darkness. It was the sound of metal on metal. Amber and her friends were cutting the bars of the fence to let the cows escape.

'It's working,' whispered Paco. 'I'm nearly there.'

Amber was cold and a little scared. It was strange to be so close to all the cows in the darkness. She could feel the heat from the heavy animals. She could see the whites of their eyes as they lifted their heads to look at her.

'Remember, everyone – if anyone comes, we run in different directions. We can meet up later,' said Andrew. 'And if you're caught, don't tell them anything!'

'This is it!' Paco said excitedly.

A piece of the fence fell to the ground. Immediately the students ran among the cows.

'Come on!' shouted Amber. 'You're free!'

The cows were confused. Why were these people running and waving their arms? They didn't like the shouting. They didn't go towards the open fence. Instead, they turned their backs on the grasslands and started moving away from it.

'What are you doing?'

Amber and the others tried to push them in the right direction. The cows were worried now. They moved closer together and they were getting louder. There was fear in the air.

'What's wrong with them?' cried Paco, over the noise.

'I don't know,' Amber shouted. 'Come on. This way!'

'Maybe they like it here …' Paco couldn't believe it.

'Don't you want to be free?' Amber whispered. 'Look! This way. This way!' she said, and she ran to the hole in the fence.

By now the cows were really frightened. They were moving quickly and nearly knocked Andrew over.

Amber was crying. 'They're going to kill you. All of you!'

Suddenly, they saw car lights coming towards them.

'Go! Go!' shouted Andrew.

Alice and Andrew started to run, but Amber couldn't leave the cows. Paco pulled her arm. 'Amber! Come on! We have to go!'

Finally, Amber ran. It wasn't right, she thought. All those cows. All one hundred thousand of them – big ones and babies – they were all going to die. Just so that people could eat a cheap burger. Amber's face was wet with tears.

* * *

In Andrew's room they were trying to understand why they had failed.

'They probably like the life behind the fences,' Andrew said thoughtfully. 'It's an easy life. You get food and water without doing anything.'

'I think they were just scared,' Amber said quietly.

Alice was angry. 'Why do the bad guys always win?'

Amber looked at her. 'Because we let them,' she said.

CHAPTER 11
Sylvia's new job

Sylvia had a job at UMP. It was her first day and she kissed Raúl goodbye. He lay on the sofa. This Raúl was very different from the Raúl she used to know. The happy, lively, optimistic Raúl had gone. Now he was quiet, angry and uncaring. His back hurt, but the worst pain was in his heart. Sylvia had to earn the money now. She had to work in that terrible place because he was too weak. In Raúl's eyes that meant he wasn't a man anymore. He couldn't look at Sylvia. Silently, she left.

* * *

In the changing room Sylvia was given white overalls, gloves and a hard hat. She followed Mike through the building. They went past the cutting room. Sylvia looked at him. Wasn't her job in there?

Mike continued walking. 'There aren't any jobs in there at the moment,' he explained. 'But I've found you a place on the killing floor.'

Sylvia suddenly felt cold. What sort of job was waiting for her there? As they got nearer to the killing floor, she began to hear different noises. They got louder. There were the noises of animals, machines and people. Then they entered a huge room and Sylvia saw the terrible truth of the killing floor.

Cows on conveyor belts were moving towards their death. They pushed and screamed in fear. An electric gun ended their screams and their dead bodies were lifted on special metal bars. Their legs were cut off and their stomachs opened with knives. Blood poured everywhere – the white floors turned to red rivers.

Sylvia couldn't move or speak. She smelt death and blood and her throat felt tight.

Mike called to a woman who was working there, 'Maggie, show Sylvia what to do.' He smiled at Sylvia. 'You'll be OK,' he said. He walked away.

'It's easier than it looks,' Maggie said, and she showed Sylvia how to reach inside the carcass and pull out certain parts.

Sylvia didn't hear her. She could only hear the noise of the cows. She could only see the blood and the broken bodies. Blood had showered her face and overalls. Tears ran red down her cheeks. Then slowly she moved her hand with the knife and copied Maggie. She reached inside the warm body and cut.

But the tears didn't stop. This was her life now. She cut meat. She was meat. Just another part of the machine.

EPILOGUE

Don looked round the meeting room. Everyone was smiling and pleased with Mickey's sales. Phil was the boss now. Jack had gone.

'So,' Phil said, 'we think that next month will be the best time for our latest idea. You're going to like this. Don?'

Don stood up and went to the front of the room where there was a large picture of a new Mickey's burger. He looked older than before and he was quieter. He had lost something in Cody, but he still had his job.

'Yes,' he said, and he pointed to the advertisement. 'As you know, we've been testing the Barbecue Big One for months. People love it. It's time to start advertising. This is an exciting moment!' His words were confident but inside he felt cold.

* * *

In the desert another group of Mexicans was making the long, hot journey across the border. This time there were two young boys in the group.

One of them found an old boot on the ground. 'Look!' he shouted excitedly.

Esteban spoke sharply to him. 'Put it down. It's bad luck.' Then he made the sign of the cross. He knew whose boot it was. Roberto's.

They arrived at the edge of the road and Benny's old yellow van was waiting for them. Benny came up to the boys, smiling. He held out two kids' meals from Mickey's.

'Hello boys,' he said. 'Welcome to the USA.'

Fast Food Nation:

*F*ast Food Nation began life as a book. It was written by the American journalist, Eric Schlosser, and it was published in 2001. In *Fast Food Nation*, Schlosser looks at the fast food industry in the US. He writes about the first ever burger bars; he visits meat packing factories and talks to the people who work there; he speaks to farmers, and to the teenagers who spend evenings and weekends working in fast food restaurants. Schlosser's book made people think about fast food, and where it comes from.

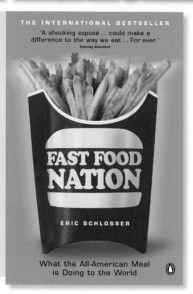

THE INTERNATIONAL BESTSELLER

'A shocking exposé ... could make a difference to the way we eat ... For ever.'
Evening Standard

FAST FOOD NATION

ERIC SCHLOSSER

What the All-American Meal is Doing to the World

In 2006, *Fast Food Nation* came out as a film.
Here, Eric Schlosser talks about his book and the film.

Eric Schlosser

Why did you write *Fast Food Nation*?

The idea for *Fast Food Nation* came from *Rolling Stone* magazine. They wanted me to write a piece about the fast food industry. They wanted to show people the truth about the food they ate.

So, I started reading about it. I used to like burgers. I used to go to McDonalds. I didn't want to laugh at the 'all-American' meal. But I was very surprised by what I read. Our love of fast food has changed so many things in America – people's working conditions, the way animals are farmed, even the whole look of some places. I realised that the fast food industry was a hidden world.

from book to film

My piece came out in two parts in *Rolling Stone*. I wanted to say a lot more and so I decided to write the book. I found a small publishers who wanted to publish it. And straight away, it sold very well …

How did *Fast Food Nation* the book become *Fast Food Nation* the film?

I spoke to lots of film-makers who wanted to make documentary films of the book, but I wasn't sure about it. I didn't want to agree to a film that I would feel uncomfortable with later. Then I met film-makers Jeremy Thomas and Richard Linklater. They suggested making a story inspired by the book, not a documentary. After almost two years of talking, we decided to go ahead.

What do you think of the film?

I'm very proud of it. It's a brave film. People like me who eat meat should see where it comes from. It's a dark film, but in the United States these are dark times.

FAST FOOD NATION

> "People who eat meat should see where it comes from."
> Do you agree or disagree with this? Discuss in pairs.

How did you choose the actors in the film?

Every actor who worked on *Fast Food Nation* did it because the subject meant something to them. For example, Avril Lavigne doesn't eat meat, and she feels strongly about that. And Wilmer Valderrama (Esteban) first came to the US when he was fourteen. He didn't speak a word of English. He knows how it feels to be alone in a strange country.

What do these words mean? You can use a dictionary.
journalist   publish   industry   conditions   documentary   inspire

The 'illegals':

the hidden workers of the United States

The US-Mexico border

Every year, thousands of people from countries such as Mexico risk everything to cross the border into the United States. When they arrive, life is hard. They may work long hours in badly-paid and dangerous jobs. They have no rights as they are not legal workers. Why do they do it, and what future is there for America's illegal workers?

There are over eleven million illegal immigrants in the US. Most of these are Mexican.

A DANGEROUS JOURNEY

The US-Mexico border is over 3,000 km long. There are lots of high fences, and the US border police watch the area closely. Immigrants walk for hours in the desert heat to find places to cross where there are no police. Some try to swim or sail across the Rio Grande. Every year, Mexicans die during the journey. This is usually because they don't have enough water.

Border police with illegal immigrants

Often Mexicans will pay a guide, called a 'coyote' in Spanish, to take them across: on foot, or by boat or van. Sometimes coyotes pay money to a border police officer to let them through.

Many immigrants are caught by the border police. They are taken to a detention centre, and later they are driven back to Mexico.

A NEW LIFE

Those immigrants who manage to cross the border are 'illegals'. You need an identity card and other legal papers to get work in America. With no 'papers', immigrants have no rights as workers. They often do the jobs that no one else wants to do. They do cleaning jobs; they work on farms; they look after children; they might work in factories ... The pay is low, but they can earn much more than in their own country. Many of them send money back to their families.

THE FUTURE

Illegal immigration is seen as a big problem in the US. Some Americans feel angry at the number of immigrants in their country. They say that immigrants are taking their jobs, and using the schools and hospitals. However, some companies in the US want illegal immigration to continue. They depend on having cheap workers.

For people with difficult lives in poor countries, the US often appears to be a land of dreams. As we see in *Fast Food Nation*, real life for the immigrants who arrive is often very different.

> **"We all share the same world. People should be able to work and live where they want."**
> **Discuss in class.**

Immigrant factory workers

What do these words mean? You can use a dictionary.
risk   illegal   legal   immigrant   detention centre   identity card

A SHORT HISTORY

Most of us eat fast food at some time in our lives. Some people might even find it hard to live without fast food restaurants. So how and why did America become a 'fast food nation'?

THE AGE OF THE CAR

In the 1940s, a new type of eating place appeared in America – the drive-in restaurant. It was designed for a changing way of life. People stayed in their cars and waitresses served them. Drive-ins were popular with teenagers.

THE MCDONALD BROTHERS

In 1940 Richard and Maurice McDonald opened the 'McDonald Brothers' Burger Bar Drive-In' in San Bernardino, California. It was near a high school, it employed twenty waitresses, and it made them rich.

Eight years later, the brothers decided it was time to change. They changed their drive-in for a different kind of restaurant where people had to line up inside for food. There were no plates or glasses; everything was made of paper. There were no waitresses and there was no washing-up. The prices were cheaper and the food arrived more quickly than in a drive-in.

OF FAST FOOD

The first ever McDonald's, now a museum

It was the first self-service restaurant and it was hugely popular. It made the McDonalds a lot of money.

Businessmen from all over America visited the San Bernardino restaurant and copied the McDonald's model in their own fast food businesses.

THE 'GOLDEN ARCHES'

Richard McDonald designed a new building for the restaurant. He wanted drivers to see it easily from the road. On the roof, he put two yellow arches in the shape of an 'M'. The famous McDonald's logo had arrived!

> How many fast food restaurants are there in your town? Do they serve American food or local food? Which ones do you prefer and why? Discuss in pairs.

AMERICA AND THE WORLD …

Between 1960 and 1973, the number of McDonald's restaurants in America grew from 250 to 3,000. Wall Street* put money into the fast food businesses. A fast food nation was born.

Today, you can find big fast food chains like McDonald's in most countries in the world. Love it or hate it, it seems that fast food is here to stay.

* Wall Street is the centre of finance in New York.

What do these words mean? You can use a dictionary.
self-service   model   arch(es)   logo   finance

Prologue–Chapter 3

Before you read

You can use your dictionary for these questions.

1 Match the words with the definition.

border   cargo   fence   lime   manure   overalls

a) This goes round a garden or a field.

b) This is carried by trucks, planes and boats.

c) You wear these to protect your clothes.

d) This is a small, green fruit.

e) This is a big farm.

f) Cows leave this on the fields.

2 Match the two halves of the sentences.

a) The woman leaned out of	**i)** my suitcase for me.
b) We had a barbecue	**ii)** shocked everyone.
c) My sister packed	**iii)** the window to say hello.
d) The company advertised	**iv)** in the garden.
e) The sudden loud noise	**v)** the new car on TV.

3 Look at People and Places on pages 4–5. Choose three people.

a) What do you think their lives are like?

b) Which person would you prefer to be? Why?

After you read

4 Complete the sentences with the correct names.

Mike   Roberto   Jack   Benny   Esteban   Harry

a) … thinks that there is a problem with Mickey's meat.

b) … works for Mickey's in Chicago.

c) … knows the way across the border.

d) … drives a yellow van.

e) … gets lost in the desert.

f) … chooses Raúl and Jorge to work at the factory.

5 What do you think?

a) Who do you like most? Why?

b) What job will Raúl and Jorge have at the factory?

c) What problems do workers at the factory have?

Chapters 4–6

Before you read

6 Match the questions and answers. You can use a dictionary.

a) What is a conveyor belt used for?   **i)** cleaning things

b) Who usually takes drugs?   **ii)** a large farm

c) What is a hose used for?   **iii)** moving things in a factory

d) What is a ranch?   **iv)** people who are ill

7 What do you think happens next? Choose the correct alternative.

a) Raúl earns *a lot of / a little* money.

b) Raúl's job is *easy / difficult*.

c) Don is *pleased / not pleased* when he visits the factory.

d) Coco *likes / doesn't like* Mike.

e) Don hears *good / bad* stories about the factory.

f) Sylvia *wants / doesn't want* to work at the factory.

g) Rudy thinks life is *better / worse* today than in the past.

After you read

8 Check your answers to Exercise 7.

9 Are these sentences true or false? Correct the false sentences.

a) Sylvia doesn't want to kiss Raúl because he's dirty.

b) Amber works at Mickey's because she likes the job.

c) The video isn't useful because it's in the wrong language.

d) Mike is angry because a worker is careless.

e) Sylvia works in the hotel because she doesn't like UMP.

f) UMP has problems because the workers aren't very good.

10 What did Harry say about these things?

a) dirt in the food

b) American people today

c) Mexican people

d) Jack

e) Don's future

11 Answer the questions.

a) What is Don's problem?

b) What did he decide?

c) Was he right? Why/Why not?

Chapter 7–Epilogue

Before you read

12 Complete the sentences with these words. You can use a dictionary.

control   environment   pollution   protest

a) People today are destroying the ...

b) Cars, planes and factories cause a lot of ...

c) Teachers need to ... their students.

d) Many people ... about things that they don't agree with.

13 Tick the things you think will happen next.

a) Coco and Mike will break up.

b) Amber will leave Mickey's.

c) There will be an accident at the factory.

d) Sylvia will become ill.

e) People will find out about the manure in the burgers.

After you read

14 Check your answers to Exercise 13.

15 Who says these things? Why?

a) 'You're not my mother!'

b) 'I don't have time for all your politics.'

c) 'Hope can kill you.'

d) 'It's all lies.'

e) 'The accident wasn't our fault.'

f) 'Don't you want to be free?'

g) 'Welcome to the USA.'

16 What do you think?

a) Do you like fast food? Why/Why not?

b) Do you think it's OK to kill animals for food?

c) Imagine you are the boss of UMP. What would you do?

d) What advice would you give to Mexican people who want to go to USA?